I READ A BOOK

TITLE: _____ TODAY: _____

I Read This Book With:
- ☐ Mom   ☐ Dad   ☐ All by myself
- ☐ My friend   ☐ My teacher   ☐ _____

This is how I feel about this book:
_____
_____
_____

My favorite part is:
_____
_____
_____
_____
_____

I would like to read it again:
☐ YES   ☐ NO   ☐ MAYBE   ☐ AGAIN AND AGAIN

I READ A BOOK

TITLE: _____   TODAY: _____

I Read This Book With:
- ☐ Mom   ☐ Dad   ☐ All by myself
- ☐ My friend   ☐ My teacher   ☐ _____

This is how I feel about this book:

_____
_____
_____
_____

My favorite part is:

_____
_____
_____
_____
_____
_____
_____

I would like to read it again:

☐ YES   ☐ NO   ☐ MAYBE   ☐ AGAIN AND AGAIN

I READ A BOOK

TITLE: _____ TODAY: _____

I Read This Book With:
- ☐ Mom   ☐ Dad   ☐ All by myself
- ☐ My friend ☐ My teacher ☐ _____

This is how I feel about this book:
_____
_____
_____

My favorite part is:
_____
_____
_____
_____
_____
_____

I would like to read it again:
☐ YES ☐ NO ☐ MAYBE ☐ AGAIN AND AGAIN

I READ A BOOK

TITLE: _____   TODAY: _____

I Read This Book With:
☐ Mom   ☐ Dad   ☐ All by myself
☐ My friend   ☐ My teacher   ☐ _____

This is how I feel about this book:
_____
_____
_____

My favorite part is:
_____
_____
_____
_____
_____
_____

I would like to read it again:
☐ YES   ☐ NO   ☐ MAYBE   ☐ AGAIN AND AGAIN

A BOOK IS A GIFT YOU CAN OPEN

AGAIN AND AGAIN

I READ A BOOK

TITLE: _____   TODAY: _____

I Read This Book With:
- ☐ Mom ☐ Dad ☐ All by myself
- ☐ My friend ☐ My teacher ☐ _____

This is how I feel about this book:
_____
_____
_____

My favorite part is:
_____
_____
_____
_____
_____
_____

I would like to read it again:
☐ YES ☐ NO ☐ MAYBE ☐ AGAIN AND AGAIN

I READ A BOOK

TITLE: _____   TODAY: _____

I Read This Book With:
- ☐ Mom   ☐ Dad   ☐ All by myself
- ☐ My friend ☐ My teacher ☐ _____

This is how I feel about this book:

_____
_____
_____

My favorite part is:

_____
_____
_____
_____
_____

I would like to read it again:

☐ YES   ☐ NO   ☐ MAYBE   ☐ AGAIN AND AGAIN

I READ A BOOK

TITLE: _____   TODAY: _____

I Read This Book With:
- ☐ Mom   ☐ Dad   ☐ All by myself
- ☐ My friend ☐ My teacher   ☐ _____

This is how I feel about this book:
_____
_____
_____

My favorite part is:
_____
_____
_____
_____
_____
_____

I would like to read it again:
☐ YES ☐ NO ☐ MAYBE ☐ AGAIN AND AGAIN

I READ A BOOK

TITLE: _____   TODAY: _____

I Read This Book With:
- ☐ Mom   ☐ Dad   ☐ All by myself
- ☐ My friend   ☐ My teacher   ☐ _____

This is how I feel about this book:
_____
_____
_____

My favorite part is:
_____
_____
_____
_____
_____

I would like to read it again:
☐ YES   ☐ NO   ☐ MAYBE   ☐ AGAIN AND AGAIN

I READ A BOOK

TITLE: _____ TODAY: _____

I Read This Book With:
- ☐ Mom
- ☐ Dad
- ☐ All by myself
- ☐ My friend
- ☐ My teacher
- ☐ _____

This is how I feel about this book:
_____
_____
_____

My favorite part is:
_____
_____
_____
_____
_____
_____

I would like to read it again:
☐ YES ☐ NO ☐ MAYBE ☐ AGAIN AND AGAIN

*The more that you read
The more you will know
The more you will know
the more placec you will go*

I READ A BOOK

TITLE: _____   TODAY: _____

I Read This Book With:
☐ Mom   ☐ Dad   ☐ All by myself
☐ My friend   ☐ My teacher   ☐ _____

This is how I feel about this book:
_____
_____
_____

My favorite part is:
_____
_____
_____
_____
_____
_____

I would like to read it again:
☐ YES ☐ NO ☐ MAYBE ☐ AGAIN AND AGAIN

This is how I feel after reading 10 books in a row:

These are the books I want to read next:

I became interested in these topics after reading the previous books:

I READ A BOOK

TITLE: _____   TODAY: _____

I Read This Book With:
- ☐ Mom   ☐ Dad   ☐ All by myself
- ☐ My friend   ☐ My teacher   ☐ _____

This is how I feel about this book:
_____
_____
_____
_____

My favorite part is:
_____
_____
_____
_____
_____
_____
_____

I would like to read it again:
☐ YES ☐ NO ☐ MAYBE ☐ AGAIN AND AGAIN

I READ A BOOK

TITLE: _____   TODAY: _____

I Read This Book With:
- ☐ Mom   ☐ Dad   ☐ All by myself
- ☐ My friend   ☐ My teacher   ☐ _____

This is how I feel about this book:

_____
_____
_____

My favorite part is:

_____
_____
_____
_____
_____
_____

I would like to read it again:

☐ YES ☐ NO ☐ MAYBE ☐ AGAIN AND AGAIN

I READ A BOOK

TITLE: _____   TODAY: _____

I Read This Book With:
☐ Mom   ☐ Dad   ☐ All by myself
☐ My friend   ☐ My teacher   ☐ _____

This is how I feel about this book:
_____
_____
_____

My favorite part is:
_____
_____
_____
_____
_____
_____

I would like to read it again:
☐ YES   ☐ NO   ☐ MAYBE   ☐ AGAIN AND AGAIN

I READ A BOOK

TITLE: _____   TODAY: _____

I Read This Book With:
- ☐ Mom   ☐ Dad   ☐ All by myself
- ☐ My friend   ☐ My teacher   ☐ _____

This is how I feel about this book:

_____
_____
_____

My favorite part is:

_____
_____
_____
_____
_____

I would like to read it again:

☐ YES   ☐ NO   ☐ MAYBE   ☐ AGAIN AND AGAIN

I READ A BOOK

TITLE: _____   TODAY: _____

I Read This Book With:
- ☐ Mom
- ☐ Dad
- ☐ All by myself
- ☐ My friend
- ☐ My teacher
- ☐ _____

This is how I feel about this book:
_____
_____
_____

My favorite part is:
_____
_____
_____
_____
_____
_____

I would like to read it again:
☐ YES   ☐ NO   ☐ MAYBE   ☐ AGAIN AND AGAIN

I READ A BOOK

TITLE: _____   TODAY: _____

I Read This Book With:
- ☐ Mom   ☐ Dad   ☐ All by myself
- ☐ My friend ☐ My teacher ☐ _____

This is how I feel about this book:
_____
_____
_____

My favorite part is:
_____
_____
_____
_____
_____

I would like to read it again:
☐ YES ☐ NO ☐ MAYBE ☐ AGAIN AND AGAIN

I READ A BOOK

TITLE: _____   TODAY: _____

I Read This Book With:
- ☐ Mom ☐ Dad ☐ All by myself
- ☐ My friend ☐ My teacher ☐ _____

This is how I feel about this book:

_____
_____
_____

My favorite part is:

_____
_____
_____
_____
_____
_____

I would like to read it again:

☐ YES   ☐ NO   ☐ MAYBE   ☐ AGAIN AND AGAIN

Draw your favorite character here:

I READ A BOOK

TITLE: _____   TODAY: _____

I Read This Book With:
- [ ] Mom   [ ] Dad   [ ] All by myself
- [ ] My friend   [ ] My teacher   [ ] _____

This is how I feel about this book:
_____
_____
_____
_____

My favorite part is:
_____
_____
_____
_____
_____
_____
_____

I would like to read it again:
[ ] YES   [ ] NO   [ ] MAYBE   [ ] AGAIN AND AGAIN

I READ A BOOK

TITLE: _____   TODAY: _____

I Read This Book With:
- ☐ Mom   ☐ Dad   ☐ All by myself
- ☐ My friend ☐ My teacher ☐ _____

This is how I feel about this book:

_____
_____
_____

My favorite part is:

_____
_____
_____
_____
_____
_____

I would like to read it again:

☐ YES   ☐ NO   ☐ MAYBE   ☐ AGAIN AND AGAIN

I READ A BOOK

TITLE: _____   TODAY: _____

I Read This Book With:
- ☐ Mom   ☐ Dad   ☐ All by myself
- ☐ My friend   ☐ My teacher   ☐ _____

This is how I feel about this book:

_____
_____
_____

My favorite part is:

_____
_____
_____
_____
_____
_____

I would like to read it again:

☐ YES   ☐ NO   ☐ MAYBE   ☐ AGAIN AND AGAIN

I READ A BOOK

TITLE: _____   TODAY: _____

I Read This Book With:
- ☐ Mom   ☐ Dad   ☐ All by myself
- ☐ My friend ☐ My teacher ☐ _____

This is how I feel about this book:

_____
_____
_____

My favorite part is:

_____
_____
_____
_____
_____
_____

I would like to read it again:

☐ YES ☐ NO ☐ MAYBE ☐ AGAIN AND AGAIN

I READ A BOOK

TITLE: _____   TODAY: _____

I Read This Book With:
- [ ] Mom   [ ] Dad   [ ] All by myself
- [ ] My friend   [ ] My teacher   [ ] _____

This is how I feel about this book:

_____
_____
_____

My favorite part is:

_____
_____
_____
_____
_____
_____

I would like to read it again:

[ ] YES   [ ] NO   [ ] MAYBE   [ ] AGAIN AND AGAIN

I READ A BOOK

TITLE: _____   TODAY: _____

I Read This Book With:
- ☐ Mom   ☐ Dad   ☐ All by myself
- ☐ My friend ☐ My teacher ☐ _____

This is how I feel about this book:

_____
_____
_____

My favorite part is:

_____
_____
_____
_____
_____
_____

I would like to read it again:

☐ YES   ☐ NO   ☐ MAYBE   ☐ AGAIN AND AGAIN

A child who
READS
Will be an adult who
THINKS

I READ A BOOK

TITLE: _____   TODAY: _____

I Read This Book With:
- [ ] Mom [ ] Dad [ ] All by myself
- [ ] My friend [ ] My teacher [ ] _____

This is how I feel about this book:
_____
_____
_____

My favorite part is:
_____
_____
_____
_____
_____
_____

I would like to read it again:
[ ] YES [ ] NO [ ] MAYBE [ ] AGAIN AND AGAIN

I READ A BOOK

TITLE: _____   TODAY: _____

I Read This Book With:
- ☐ Mom
- ☐ Dad
- ☐ All by myself
- ☐ My friend
- ☐ My teacher
- ☐ _____

This is how I feel about this book:
_____
_____
_____

My favorite part is:
_____
_____
_____
_____
_____
_____

I would like to read it again:
☐ YES ☐ NO ☐ MAYBE ☐ AGAIN AND AGAIN

Made in the USA
Lexington, KY
21 May 2017